Stinking Thinking

About the pamphlet
This pamphlet addresses the characteristic thinking that usually leads a recovering person down the road to relapse. Various specific attitudes are described in detail, with questionnaires to help readers assess their own tendencies toward these attitudes, and practical, workable solutions are suggested.

About the author
Gayle Rosellini is a freelance writer whose works on chemical dependency and other health and personal development topics have appeared in *Alcoholism/The National Magazine, U.S. Journal,* and a number of other periodicals. She is also coauthor of the book *Of Course You're Angry,* published by Hazelden.

Hazelden Classics for Clients

Stinking Thinking

Gayle Rosellini

Hazelden Publishing
hazelden.org/bookstore
800-328-9000

To request permission, write to Permissions Coordinator, Hazelden, P.O. Box 176, Center City, MN 55012-0176. To purchase additional copies of this publication, call 1-800-328-9000 or 1-651-213-4000.

Any stories or case studies that may be used in this material are composites of many individuals. Names and details have been changed to protect identities.

ISBN-13: 978-0-89486-326-4

Cover and interior design by David Spohn
Typesetting by Tursso Companies

INTRODUCTION

We *can* achieve and enjoy lasting sobriety. We have within us the potential to grow and mature in our recovery, to realize an abundant and full life. We can become people of high self-esteem and positive expectations. We can become winners.

How many recover? How many manage to stay sober and straight after their first experience in treatment? How many relapse, plunging back into the disease and desperation of chemical dependency?

The fact is, chemical dependency is a disease characterized by relapse. Of those who sincerely attempt to get sober and straight through professional counseling and Alcoholics Anonymous or Narcotics Anonymous, about 40 percent find themselves hopelessly sliding backward into chronic alcohol or other drug dependence.

What's the matter with them? Are they stupid?

Not likely. You see, lasting recovery isn't dependent on brains. The world is full of smart alcoholics and other drug addicts. A Ph.D. in nuclear physics won't guarantee a happy sobriety. Neither will winning the lottery nor coming in first in a beauty contest.

It's not intelligence or luck or good looks that keep us sober—*attitude* makes the difference in recovery.

ATTITUDE IS THE ANSWER

Attitudes are either a path to healthy and happy recovery or the road to relapse. It's that simple. This isn't a new idea at all. The ancient Greeks understood it. Norman Vincent Peale changed the lives of thousands by suggesting the power of positive thinking. Earl Nightingale told us, "We, literally, become what we think about most of the time."

Unfortunately, those of us who are recovering from chemical dependency too often suffer from what AA members call *stinking thinking*. Stinking thinking is a bad attitude. It's being negative, blaming, and chronically dissatisfied. And it's sneaky.

Our bad attitudes can be fouling the whole neighborhood, but arrogance and false pride fool us into believing our own stinking thoughts and actions are as sweet as spring flowers. It must be the other person who's raising the stench! That's another element of stinking thinking. We become experts at taking the next person's inventory while remaining blind to our own defects.

Stinking thinking is a major symptom of chemical dependency. We all suffer from it at one time or another, and it doesn't go away with thirty days of treatment. It can dog our heels even when we're sober—wrecking our recovery.

The 40 percent who slide into chronic relapse are stinking thinkers par excellence. Each of us must examine our own thinking. Is our attitude positive and constructive, or do we practice stinking thinking? Are we courting relapse with negative attitudes? Are we hanging on to sobriety with clenched teeth and fierce unhappiness?

In order to have a successful recovery, to feel good mentally and physically, we need to get our heads screwed on straight with clear and rational thinking. To do that, we need to recognize our patterns of stinking thinking and to learn ways to change those negative patterns to positive ones.

There are four common denominators that seem to characterize people who slide back into drinking or other chemical dependency. These four attitudinal qualities can appear during any stage of the recovery process, even after several years of successful sobriety, but they take an especially big toll during the critical first months of sobriety.

These attitudes are often the root cause of relapse that occurs during the first year after treatment. A person can graduate from a treatment program and still be a stinking thinker! Because, you see, weeks of intensive treatment are only the *beginning* of recovery. Recovery is a process. It takes time and effort. Recovery continues outside the treatment setting as we work to develop positive attitudes in the outside world, as we improve relationships and regain health. Recovery is dynamic. It is the process of changing and growing and maturing. For us, recovery is life.

So, let's take a closer look at the stinking attitudes that can stop recovery in its tracks.

Lip Service

Fyodor Dostoyevsky, the Russian novelist, once observed, "Shamming so easily coexists with sincere feeling."

His words aptly describe a phenomenon common among people being treated for chemical dependency. The phenomenon is called *lip service,* and it is a prime example of stinking thinking.

Lip service is the mouthing of insincere statements. It's telling other people what they want to hear. It's superficial compliance—a sham to make ourselves look good.

Lip service is different from lying. When we lie, we are committing an out-and-out fraud. We know we're being untruthful, and we hope we don't get caught. Lip service is more like wishful thinking. At a minimum, we half-believe what we're saying. Sometimes we're totally sincere—at the moment, anyway. But we lack follow-through. We're all talk and no action. And that's what makes lip service dangerous to recovering people. We sit around flapping our lips, wishing our words will come true.

But talk is cheap. Recovery requires action! Change! Commitment! Work!

Lip service endangers sobriety because we are naive enough to believe that repeating the right words and slogans can be an adequate substitute for the often painful and difficult job of looking into ourselves and changing the faulty beliefs and behaviors that have made our lives unmanageable.

Lip service won't work. We might be able to fool our counselor, spouse, boss, friends, or probation officer with our glib words, but unless we follow up those words with sincere action, we face the distinct possibility of relapse!

Certain key phrases are characteristic of lip service:
- I promise I'll never do it again.
- I've really learned my lesson this time.
- I think AA is great, but . . .
- Getting busted for drunk driving was the best thing that ever happened to me, your honor.
- I know I'll never drink again.
- I'm going to quit (smoking, driving without a license, eating junk, losing my temper, etc.) just as soon as . . .
- I'll do whatever you say, just don't (fire me, divorce me, put me in jail).

Remember, we usually believe our own lip service. Follow-through is what distinguishes the sham of lip service from the sincerity of true commitment to recovery. It's not what we *say* that counts. It's what we *do*.

We should ask ourselves the following questions:

1. Do I make lists of things to do or ways to improve myself, yet consistently fail to accomplish the things on my list?
2. Do I secretly believe that, although other chemically dependent people may need to follow the requirements of a treatment program to recover, those requirements don't really apply to my situation?
3. Do I sometimes find myself repeating certain phrases and slogans about my recovery in the hope of winning the approval of the people around me?
4. Do I make promises to improve my behavior that don't come true?

If we answered yes to even one of these questions, we're sabotaging our recovery by engaging in lip service.

What motivates us to sabotage ourselves this way? For one thing, we tend to be *pleasers*. We want to win the approval of our counselors, peers, and family, so we tell them what we think they want to hear. It makes them happy and they're nice to us, and that makes us happy— in the short run, anyway.

There's another, more selfish, reason we use lip service. It's an effective means of getting people off our backs. If we mouth the right slogan, we can quiet the counselor, judge, or spouse who keeps nagging at us.

The hallmark of lip service is insincerity. We get others to fall for our malarkey time after time. And that leads us to another one of our attitude problems, namely . . .

Grandiosity

Grandiosity is the flip side of low self-esteem. It is characterized by an overinflated sense of self, and those of us who suffer from it possess an embarrassingly unrealistic sense of our importance, talents, and abilities. We behave as if we are immune to the ordinary laws of the universe that govern mere mortals. We think of ourselves as, well, different.

It's our grandiose belief that other people are too dumb to recognize our insincerity that paves the way for the continued game of lip service.

Grandiosity is believing we can continue going to dark, smoky barrooms without being tempted to drink.

Grandiosity is believing we can continue running around with our old drug-using friends without being sucked back into our addiction.

Grandiosity is believing other people may need the crutch of AA or NA, but we don't need any of that spirituality crap.

Grandiosity is believing one beer or one toke isn't going to make us lose control.

Grandiosity is believing we can become social drinkers or controlled drug users again.

Grandiosity is believing we are better, smarter, or more worthy than others.

Grandiosity is believing rules are for fools, not us.

Grandiosity is the unrealistic belief that somehow, some way, we can magically beat the odds, that we can remain lazy and demanding, and not risk relapse.

Grandiosity is stinking thinking.

We must ask ourselves the following questions:

1. Do I intend to frequent bars because I know I'm strong enough not to be tempted to drink again?
2. Do I think I could probably go back to social drinking or other moderate drug use if I wanted to?
3. Do I think all those Twelve Step meetings and follow-up sessions with my counselor are too time-consuming to bother with?
4. Does being around all those alcoholics and addicts and losers at AA and NA and in the follow-up groups give me the creeps?

If we answered yes to even one of these questions, we are sabotaging our recovery with unrealistic grandiosity.

It's a paradox, but alcoholics and other addicts can be grandiose while suffering from an inferiority complex. Depending on our mood and situation, we flip-flop between the false pride and overinflated ego of grandiosity and the shattering self-hatred of depression and low self-esteem.

That's because the hallmark of both low self-esteem and grandiosity is *contempt*. With low self-esteem the contempt is aimed inward; with grandiosity, we aim outward, at other people and the rules of society and nature.

When we start to think that the rules don't apply to us, we develop a new attitude problem. It's called . . .

Corner-Cutting

It's Saturday morning, and the sun is shining, the birds are singing, and it's a beautiful day. Now, what would it hurt to skip that follow-up meeting with our counselor at the treatment center? Didn't we skip our AA meeting last week with no bad results? Besides, on a day like today, it's probably more healthy to be out in the sunshine instead of being cooped up inside a stupid building. I mean, what's the big deal with all this follow-up stuff?

The big deal is that the success of our recovery depends a great deal on our commitment to remaining active in follow-up. When we begin to miss appointments, skip meetings, and make excuses, when we become less meticulous in our commitment to recovery, we are beginning to cut corners.

Corner-cutting is a form of cheating. It usually starts small, but it can rapidly develop into a full-blown relapse. My friend Marvin is a good example of a corner-cutter.

Marvin entered an inpatient treatment program because his life was falling apart from too much alcohol and other drugs. He came out of treatment a new man, totally gung-ho, enthusiastically looking forward to a sober lifestyle. In fact, he was so excited about sobriety, he hoped to someday become a counselor himself so he could help other people. He decided to take a night class in psychology at the local community college. That's when the trouble started.

The demands of his job and family didn't leave much time for homework, especially when three nights a week were devoted to AA meetings. Something had to give. Figuring he'd get just as much out of the psychology class as he would AA, Marvin cut his AA meetings down to once a week. Then he stopped going altogether, but he still tried to read his Big Book about once a week. About a month later, Marvin's wife, Stella, began to complain about the lack of time they spent together, so Marvin surprised her by canceling their family counseling session at the treatment center and treating her to a prime rib dinner at the best restaurant in town.

Actually, Marvin was feeling pretty guilty about spending so many evenings away from home, and he hoped the fancy dinner would stop Stella's complaining. He was pretty sure she was getting suspicious, but Marvin didn't think he was doing anything so bad. A guy had the right to see his old friends, didn't he? And he was staying almost totally straight. He could be snorting cocaine every night if he wanted, but he'd turned it down every single time it was offered. A few tokes off a joint, that's the most he ever did. What could it hurt? The stuff was practically harmless. He never even really got high from it.

What could it hurt?

Within three months, Marvin was totally down the tubes. His corner-cutting, his succession of small cheats caught up with him, resulting in a total relapse.

Corner-cutting is insidious. Our first cheats seem small and innocent, certainly no cause for concern. And we always have a good explanation for our deviation. Unless we recognize corner-cutting for the stinking thinking it is, it inevitably leads to disaster.

We should ask ourselves these questions:

1. Have I skipped a counseling session or AA meeting because I was too tired or busy, or because I felt I was doing so well I didn't need it?
2. Have I taken a drink or other drug even once?
3. Am I ignoring certain instructions from my counselor or doctor regarding diet, exercise, stress management, homework assignments, etc., because it's too much trouble?
4. Have I neglected to take my moral inventory on a regular basis or have I avoided taking positive action to correct my character defects?

If we answered yes to even one of these questions, we're sabotaging our recovery with corner-cutting.

The hallmark of corner-cutting is *excuse-making*.

We can become quite skillful at combining lip service, grandiosity, and corner-cutting together to form a monumentally bad attitude that endangers our recovery. An example of our stinking thinking might sound like this:

"Hey, I think Alcoholics Anonymous is really great (lip service), but I'm not the kind of person who needs all that group reinforcement to stay sober (grandiosity). Besides, I need to spend all the extra time I can with my family to make up for the way I neglected them when I was drinking (excuse-making)."

In the normal course of events, family and friends will begin to notice the corner-cutting. They'll get worried. And they'll start to nag, which brings out our defiance.

Defiance

As a group, alcoholics and other addicts are a defiant lot. We just can't stand to be told what to do. The minute someone starts ordering us around (even if they're right, even if it's for our own good), our hackles raise.

For us, defiance is as normal as breathing. We seem to possess a natural will to resist and oppose authority figures. And to us, an authority figure can be anyone, including our spouse, our kids, our parents, our counselor, and our AA sponsor. It's anyone who tries to influence our behavior.

Perhaps our defiance stems partly from our grandiosity. We always want to be right. Our grandiosity deceives us into believing that we have all the answers, that everything would be just fine if all these other stupid people would do things our way.

Of course, we don't always display our defiance openly. We may even appear perfectly pleasant and agreeable on the outside, but on the inside we're plotting and scheming to get our own way and do exactly as we please.

Because of our defiance and grandiosity, we're not very good at taking advice from counselors and other recovering people who know the score, who could help us if we'd only listen instead of filtering everything through our overinflated egos.

We should ask ourselves the following questions:

1. Do I feel like other people are always trying to run my life?
2. Do I make promises to improve my behavior when I actually have no real intention of changing?
3. Do I sometimes feel that my counselor or sponsor is a fool, or worse?

If we answered yes to even one of these questions, we are sabotaging our recovery with defiance.

The hallmark of defiance is *immaturity*. In many ways, we are like big babies. We want to be the center of attention, and we want to have all our needs met immediately. We become angry and resentful when the people around us don't act the way we wish. We start to blame them for all our problems, and we expend an enormous amount of energy trying to get them to change, to act right, to make us happy.

That's what makes defiance so dangerous to our recovery. We're so busy defiantly trying to control and change other people, we don't have enough energy or insight left to change ourselves and our stinking thinking.

A good attitude is the answer! Recovery flourishes when we fearlessly examine our thoughts and actions, when we dedicate ourselves to recognizing and eliminating the destructive habits of lip service, grandiosity, corner-cutting, and defiance.

These four attitudinal qualities foster destructive beliefs that can make our lives unmanageable and miserable, even if we're sober.

But we can change! We can challenge our stinking thinking; we can learn new and healthy responses to life. We can get our heads screwed on straight.

CHALLENGING OUR STINKING THINKING

At least three things are necessary to challenge stinking thinking.

Awareness

We can't change a bad attitude if we're not aware of it, and as long as we bury our heads in the sand of grandiosity and defiance, we'll never recognize our own character defects. The Fourth Step of Alcoholics Anonymous is an excellent way to increase our awareness of our behaviors.

Awareness can be painful. We have a natural tendency to deny our shortcomings, protect our egos, and shield ourselves from the awful truth of our mistakes. But without awareness, we can never grow or improve.

So, let's be fearless in our moral inventory! Once we get past the initial pain of searching our souls, we may just find self-awareness wonderfully liberating.

Commitment

Now is not the time for superficial lip service. Positive change requires hard work and practice. We must seek out wise counsel in the form of a skilled therapist, a trusted sponsor, a caring fellowship.

We must examine our plans for improving ourselves. Are we already cutting corners? Taking the easy way out? Change doesn't come easily, but aren't we worth the effort? Sincere commitment to our recovery is vital!

Action

Self-awareness is meaningless unless we take positive and constructive action to improve our weaknesses and bolster our strengths. We possess the remarkable ability to change, yet our insights are often followed by inactivity. Why?

Fear can stop us: fear of the unknown, fear of facing ourselves. "It might hurt," we say. "Change scares me." Laziness is a big block. "Why bother?" we ask. "I've survived this long without changing." And grandiosity, coupled with low self-esteem, keeps us stuck in our rut. "I don't need to change," we insist, afraid to admit our weakness. "There's nothing wrong with me!"

Action makes the difference between success and failure. If we're ready to change, to improve and grow, now is the time to go for it.

TRANSFORMATIONS

The most important point to remember about stinking thinking is this: *We can choose our attitudes!*

We can be grumpy or we can be positive. The choice is ours to make! By eliminating stinking thinking, we are thinking clearly and committing ourselves to recovery.

We've already learned about the hallmarks of relapse—insincerity, contempt, excuse-making, and immaturity. These personality characteristics are stumbling blocks in our search for happiness and maturity.

But with awareness, commitment, and action, we can transform these stumbling blocks into the building blocks of recovery! We can counterbalance these negative aspects of our personality by actively striving toward the *positive opposites* of these characteristics.

Let's take a look at the positive opposites that can enhance our recovery. On one side are the negative characteristics that pave the way to relapse; on the other side we see the positive opposites, the personality traits that signal a winning attitude and a healthy recovery.

Symptoms of Relapse vs.	Signs of Recovery
LIP SERVICE	COMMITMENT
Hallmark: Insincerity	*Hallmark:* Sincerity
False	Genuine
Deceitful	Honest
Hypocritical	Candid
Pretending	Serious
Exaggerating	Trustworthy
Sneaky	Sincere
All talk	Active
Fickle	Dedicated
GRANDIOSITY	SELF-CONFIDENCE
Hallmark: Contempt	*Hallmark:* Respect
Loud-mouthed	Listening
Pompous	Humble
Accusing	Understanding
Egotistical	Considerate
Ignorant	Learning
Self-hating	Self-loving
Arrogant	Assured
Fantasizing	Realistic

CORNER-CUTTING	VIGILANT
Hallmark: Excuse-making	*Hallmark:* Accountable
Irresponsible	Responsible
Lazy	Energetic
Passive	Active
Unreliable	Scrupulous
Self-indulgent	Disciplined
Impulsive	Self-controlled
Late	Punctual
Devious	True

DEFIANCE	ACCEPTANCE
Hallmark: Immaturity	*Hallmark:* Maturity
Demanding	Giving
Stubborn	Open-minded
Self-centered	Caring
Angry	Calm
Frightened	Open to change
Argumentative	Questioning
Resisting	Surrendering
Rigid	Flexible

Now, let's take a look at ourselves, a close and honest look at our innermost thoughts and feelings.

Which list of personality characteristics best describes the way we'd like to be?

Which list best describes the way we've been and the way we are now?

Have we become insincere, egotistical, unreliable, and demanding? Have we been deceitful, arrogant, irresponsible, and argumentative? Is our thinking clear and rational or are we bogged down in the mire of stinking thinking?

NOW IS THE TIME FOR CLEAR THINKING

Clear thinking is a sign of recovery. Stinking thinking signals relapse. Clear thinkers are self-aware. They readily admit their perceptions and behavior have been shaded and muddled by their addictive disease. They are not afraid or ashamed to admit their faults and weaknesses because they know they possess the potential to transform their faults into the positive opposites that can enhance their recovery. Clear thinkers are honest—not just with other people. They are honest with themselves. They are honest about their disease and about the time and effort that positive recovery requires. They know they don't have all the answers, and they accept that they can't always be right.

Clear thinkers are eager to learn—especially about their potential to recover from their addictive disease and to lead a healthy and happy life.

Stinking thinkers are unaware. They feel like victims, denying the role their own behavior plays in their problems. They are selfishly unaware of the needs of others and unaware of the impact their behavior has on their loved ones.

Clear thinkers accept responsibility for their recovery.

Stinking thinkers blame their problems on others. Clear thinkers are open-minded.

Stinking thinkers are closed, frightened, defensive.

Which are we? Are we clear thinkers or stinking thinkers? Can we agree or disagree with these statements?

1. I'm proud of my ability to talk myself out of tight spots.
2. Counseling has failed for me because I discovered I was smarter than my counselor.

3. I don't need a support group to stay straight because I've learned just about everything I need to know, and I'll be able to spot any trouble signs if they come up.
4. Half my problems would be solved if other people would get off my case and treat me right.

Could we agree with even one of these statements? Could we recognize the symptoms of insecurity, arrogance, rationalizing, and self-centeredness implicit in these statements?

REMEMBER: The first and most important step to clear thinking is *awareness*.

In recovery, we seek and walk with awareness every day of our lives, opening ourselves to new experiences and healthy methods of coping with life's problems. We don't run or hide; we don't lie and bluster. We humbly accept the responsibility for our own well-being, vigilantly examining our daily behavior for symptoms of stinking thinking and relapse.

All we really need to do to become clear thinkers is to learn to ask ourselves a few questions: "Am I being honest?" "Am I being realistic?" "Am I being accountable for my actions?" "Am I being accepting and open?"

These questions challenge stinking thinking. If we can answer yes, or if we're willing to seek the wise counsel of someone who is experienced in clear thinking, we have the solid footing we need for recovery.

With this awareness, we can commit ourselves to positive action. We can transform ourselves, with each new day. We can recover!

About Hazelden Publishing

As part of the Hazelden Betty Ford Foundation, Hazelden Publishing offers both cutting-edge educational resources and inspirational books. Our print and digital works help guide individuals in treatment and recovery, and their loved ones. Professionals who work to prevent and treat addiction also turn to Hazelden Publishing for evidence-based curricula, digital content solutions, and videos for use in schools, treatment programs, correctional programs, and electronic health records systems. We also offer training for implementation of our curricula.

Through published and digital works, Hazelden Publishing extends the reach of healing and hope to individuals, families, and communities affected by addiction and related issues.

For more information about Hazelden publications,
please call **800-328-9000**
or visit us online at **hazelden.org/bookstore**.